Margo Pargo, pudding pie,
you're the apple of my eye.

The Secret Skills of Margo Pargo:
Potty Professional

Written by: Melissa Sue Walker
Illustrated by: Winda Mulyasari

Copyright Margo Pargo Books, 2020.

Margo Pargo Books is an imprint of Running Hills Press.

All rights reserved. This book or any portion thereof may not be reproduced or used in any manner whatsoever without the express written permission of the publisher except for the use of brief quotations in a book review.

Printed in the United States of America
First Printing, 2020
ISBN: 978-1-951673-00-0

www.margopargobooks.com

I'm so glad you came over to play. You will never believe what happened to me yesterday. Can you guess?

Well, I'll tell you.
I got...

potty trained!

It all started when Grandma came to visit. She said it was time for me to start using the potty. Mom did *not* agree.

"Margo Pargo is just a *baby*!" she said. "She couldn't possibly know how to sit on the potty yet."

What? Didn't know how to sit on the potty?
Of *course* I knew how.

I was just used to wearing diapers, that's all.

Honestly, I thought everyone knew I was a big kid. Could a baby count to ten? Could a baby eat gummy bears?

Could a baby stand on one foot or jump off the couch into a pile of pillows?

No, but I could.
And I was no baby.

I didn't even need my diaper station any more. We could send my diapers to the hospital for the newborn babies.

I could use the shelf space for my favorite toys!

I was ready to ditch the diapers for good, I grabbed my favorite hot pink undies and marched straight to the bathroom.

"Where do you think you're going?" Mom asked.

"To the potty," I replied and kept on walking.

"Oh, Margo Pargo. You're still too little for the potty," Mom explained. "You can use diapers until you get bigger, and *then* you can use the potty."

One thing was clear: I had to show Mom my *secret skills*. I headed to the kitchen and filled my tummy with as much water and fishy crackers as it could hold.

After all, everyone knows what happens to the food you put in your tummy…right?

Can you guess what happened next?

That's right...

Potty time!

I called Mom and Grandma over for the big event.

"Shhh - *listen!*" I said.

They could hardly believe their ears!

The proof was in the potty.

Mom said I should do the honors.

There you have it! No grown-up is going to tell *me* that I can't use the potty.

I.

Am.

Big.

And when **you** grow big, you'll use the potty too!

What **BIG KID** things can **YOU** do?

	Yep!	Maybe Soon!
Count to ten?	☐	☐
Eat gummy bears?	☐	☐
Stand on one foot?	☐	☐
Jump off the couch?	☐	☐
Blow bubbles?	☐	☐
Host a play date?	☐	☐
Sing the ABCs?	☐	☐
Build a sand castle?	☐	☐
Make a blanket fort?	☐	☐
Drink with a straw?	☐	☐
Wink one eye?	☐	☐
Color pictures?	☐	☐

What else?

A Note to Parents:

In *The Secret Skills of Margo Pargo: Potty Professional*, Margo Pargo decides she is ready to start using the potty because she believes she is a big kid - and is eager to surprise and impress the adults in her life. She also understands some basics about the business of being human: we eat, we drink, we go potty. She even notices that when we use the potty, we can hear and see our success: *"Shhh - listen!"* she tells her family.

Margo Pargo makes the connection that many of the amazing things she can do (standing on one foot, counting to ten, etc.) are sure signs that she is getting bigger. So when she makes up her mind to use the potty, there is no stopping her.

When it comes to teaching a child to use the potty, there is no one-size-fits-all method. Every child is on his or her own timeline. By staying positive and thinking through a developmentally appropriate approach, you will allow your child to take the lead - just like a big kid.

Find us on **Amazon**, and let us know what you think!

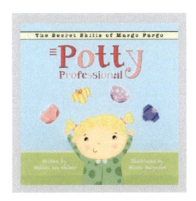

Now on Amazon

February 2020

March 2020

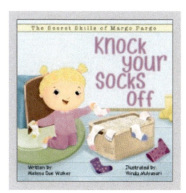

Spring 2020

RUNNING HILLS PRESS

Made in the USA
Monee, IL
17 October 2020